50 Small Bites Recipes for Home

By: Kelly Johnson

Table of Contents

- Caprese Skewers
- Mini Spinach and Feta Quiches
- Stuffed Mushrooms with Garlic and Herb Cream Cheese
- Bacon-Wrapped Dates
- Shrimp Cocktail Shots
- Bruschetta with Tomato and Basil
- Mini Meatballs with Dipping Sauce
- Spinach Artichoke Dip Bites
- Pigs in a Blanket
- Goat Cheese and Fig Crostini
- Deviled Eggs with Smoked Paprika
- Asian Meatballs with Soy Glaze
- Cheese and Charcuterie Board
- Mini Tacos with Avocado Salsa
- Sweet Potato Bites with Maple Glaze
- Hummus and Veggie Cups
- Smoked Salmon and Cream Cheese Wraps
- Mini Caprese Salad Cups
- Thai Chicken Satay Skewers
- Mini Grilled Cheese Sandwiches
- Jalapeño Poppers with Cream Cheese
- Olive Tapenade on Crostini
- Buffalo Cauliflower Bites
- Mini Quiches Lorraine
- Sesame Crusted Ahi Tuna Bites
- Roasted Red Pepper Hummus Pinwheels
- Cheesy Garlic Breadsticks
- Coconut Shrimp with Mango Dipping Sauce
- Tomato Basil Bruschetta with Balsamic Glaze
- Antipasto Skewers
- Mini BBQ Chicken Sliders
- Cucumber Bites with Dill Cream Cheese
- Spicy Tuna Tartare on Wonton Chips
- Eggplant Caponata on Crostini
- Parmesan Crisps with Whipped Goat Cheese
- Caramelized Onion and Gruyère Tartlets

- Zucchini Fritters with Yogurt Sauce
- Fruit and Cheese Skewers
- Curried Chicken Salad in Endive Leaves
- Baked Brie with Cranberries and Pecans
- Mini Corn Dogs with Mustard Dip
- Roasted Garlic and White Bean Dip
- Veggie Spring Rolls with Peanut Dipping Sauce
- Mini Pesto and Mozzarella Flatbreads
- Sweet and Spicy Meatballs
- Mushroom and Swiss Sliders
- Chocolate-Dipped Strawberries
- Avocado Deviled Eggs
- Beet and Goat Cheese Salad Bites
- Lemon Basil Shrimp Cups

Caprese Skewers

Ingredients:

- Cherry tomatoes
- Fresh mozzarella balls (bocconcini)
- Fresh basil leaves
- Balsamic glaze (optional)
- Olive oil (optional)
- Salt and pepper (to taste)
- Skewers or toothpicks

Instructions:

1. **Prepare the Ingredients**: Rinse cherry tomatoes and basil leaves. Drain mozzarella balls if packed in water.
2. **Assemble the Skewers**: On each skewer, thread a cherry tomato, a basil leaf, and a mozzarella ball. Repeat until filled, leaving space at the ends.
3. **Drizzle and Season**: Arrange skewers on a platter. Drizzle with olive oil and balsamic glaze, if desired, and sprinkle with salt and pepper.
4. **Serve**: Enjoy fresh as a delightful appetizer!

Mini Spinach and Feta Quiches

Ingredients:

- 1 cup fresh spinach, chopped
- 1/2 cup feta cheese, crumbled
- 4 large eggs
- 1/2 cup milk
- 1/4 teaspoon salt
- 1/4 teaspoon pepper
- 1 teaspoon olive oil
- 1 package phyllo dough or pre-made mini pastry shells

Instructions:

1. **Preheat the Oven**: Preheat to 375°F (190°C).
2. **Sauté Spinach**: In a skillet, heat olive oil over medium heat. Add chopped spinach and sauté until wilted. Remove from heat and let cool.
3. **Mix Filling**: In a bowl, whisk together eggs, milk, salt, and pepper. Stir in the cooled spinach and crumbled feta.
4. **Prepare Pastry Shells**: If using phyllo dough, layer sheets and cut into squares. Press into a greased muffin tin. If using pre-made shells, place them directly in the tin.
5. **Fill and Bake**: Pour the spinach mixture into each pastry shell. Bake for 20-25 minutes or until the egg is set and tops are golden.
6. **Serve**: Let cool slightly before serving warm.

Stuffed Mushrooms with Garlic and Herb Cream Cheese

Ingredients:

- 16 large cremini or button mushrooms
- 8 oz cream cheese, softened
- 2 cloves garlic, minced
- 1/4 cup fresh parsley, chopped
- 1/4 cup grated Parmesan cheese
- 1 teaspoon Italian seasoning
- Salt and pepper (to taste)
- Olive oil (for drizzling)

Instructions:

1. **Preheat the Oven**: Preheat to 375°F (190°C).
2. **Prepare Mushrooms**: Remove stems from mushrooms and set caps aside. Finely chop the stems.
3. **Make Filling**: In a bowl, mix cream cheese, minced garlic, chopped mushroom stems, parsley, Parmesan cheese, Italian seasoning, salt, and pepper until well combined.
4. **Stuff Mushrooms**: Fill each mushroom cap with the cream cheese mixture and place them on a baking sheet.
5. **Drizzle and Bake**: Drizzle with olive oil and bake for 20 minutes or until golden and bubbly.
6. **Serve**: Enjoy warm as a delicious appetizer!

Enjoy these tasty bites at your next gathering!

Bacon-Wrapped Dates

Ingredients:

- 12 Medjool dates, pitted
- 6 slices of bacon, cut in half
- Toothpicks

Instructions:

1. **Preheat the Oven**: Preheat to 400°F (200°C).
2. **Wrap Dates**: Wrap each date with half a slice of bacon and secure with a toothpick.
3. **Bake**: Place on a baking sheet and bake for 20-25 minutes, or until the bacon is crispy.
4. **Serve**: Let cool slightly before serving warm.

Shrimp Cocktail Shots

Ingredients:

- 12 cooked shrimp, peeled and deveined
- 1 cup cocktail sauce
- 12 shot glasses
- Lemon wedges (for garnish)

Instructions:

1. **Layer Sauce**: Place a spoonful of cocktail sauce in the bottom of each shot glass.
2. **Add Shrimp**: Stand a shrimp upright in each glass.
3. **Garnish**: Add a lemon wedge on the rim of each glass.
4. **Serve**: Enjoy chilled!

Bruschetta with Tomato and Basil

Ingredients:

- 1 baguette, sliced
- 2 cups diced tomatoes
- 1/4 cup fresh basil, chopped
- 2 cloves garlic, minced
- 2 tablespoons olive oil
- Salt and pepper (to taste)

Instructions:

1. **Toast Bread**: Preheat oven to 400°F (200°C). Place baguette slices on a baking sheet and toast for 5-7 minutes.
2. **Mix Topping**: In a bowl, combine tomatoes, basil, garlic, olive oil, salt, and pepper.
3. **Top Bread**: Spoon the tomato mixture onto toasted baguette slices.
4. **Serve**: Enjoy immediately!

Mini Meatballs with Dipping Sauce

Ingredients:

- 1 lb ground beef or turkey
- 1/2 cup breadcrumbs
- 1/4 cup grated Parmesan cheese
- 1 egg
- 1 teaspoon Italian seasoning
- Marinara sauce (for dipping)

Instructions:

1. **Preheat the Oven**: Preheat to 375°F (190°C).
2. **Mix Ingredients**: In a bowl, combine ground meat, breadcrumbs, Parmesan, egg, and Italian seasoning.
3. **Form Meatballs**: Roll mixture into small meatballs and place on a baking sheet.
4. **Bake**: Bake for 20-25 minutes until cooked through.
5. **Serve**: Serve with warm marinara sauce for dipping.

Spinach Artichoke Dip Bites

Ingredients:

- 1 cup spinach, cooked and chopped
- 1 cup artichoke hearts, chopped
- 1 cup cream cheese, softened
- 1/2 cup sour cream
- 1/2 cup grated Parmesan cheese
- Mini phyllo pastry cups

Instructions:

1. **Preheat the Oven**: Preheat to 375°F (190°C).
2. **Mix Filling**: In a bowl, combine spinach, artichokes, cream cheese, sour cream, and Parmesan.
3. **Fill Cups**: Spoon mixture into mini phyllo cups.
4. **Bake**: Bake for 15-20 minutes until heated through.
5. **Serve**: Enjoy warm!

Pigs in a Blanket

Ingredients:

- 1 package crescent roll dough
- 12 mini sausages
- Mustard or ketchup (for dipping)

Instructions:

1. **Preheat the Oven**: Preheat to 375°F (190°C).
2. **Roll Dough**: Unroll crescent roll dough and cut into triangles. Wrap each mini sausage with a piece of dough.
3. **Bake**: Place on a baking sheet and bake for 12-15 minutes until golden brown.
4. **Serve**: Enjoy with dipping sauces!

Goat Cheese and Fig Crostini

Ingredients:

- 1 baguette, sliced
- 4 oz goat cheese, softened
- 1/2 cup fig jam
- Fresh thyme (for garnish)

Instructions:

1. **Toast Bread**: Preheat oven to 400°F (200°C). Toast baguette slices for 5-7 minutes.
2. **Spread Cheese**: Spread a layer of goat cheese on each slice.
3. **Top with Jam**: Add a spoonful of fig jam on top of the cheese.
4. **Garnish**: Top with fresh thyme before serving.

Deviled Eggs with Smoked Paprika

Ingredients:

- 6 hard-boiled eggs
- 3 tablespoons mayonnaise
- 1 teaspoon mustard
- Salt and pepper (to taste)
- Smoked paprika (for garnish)

Instructions:

1. **Prepare Eggs**: Halve hard-boiled eggs and remove yolks.
2. **Mix Filling**: In a bowl, mash yolks with mayonnaise, mustard, salt, and pepper.
3. **Fill Eggs**: Spoon or pipe the mixture back into egg whites.
4. **Garnish**: Sprinkle with smoked paprika before serving.

Enjoy these delicious appetizers at your next gathering!

Asian Meatballs with Soy Glaze

Ingredients:

- 1 lb ground chicken or pork
- 1/4 cup breadcrumbs
- 2 green onions, chopped
- 2 cloves garlic, minced
- 1 tablespoon ginger, grated
- 1/4 cup soy sauce
- 2 tablespoons honey
- 1 tablespoon sesame oil
- Sesame seeds (for garnish)

Instructions:

1. **Preheat the Oven**: Preheat to 400°F (200°C).
2. **Mix Ingredients**: In a bowl, combine ground meat, breadcrumbs, green onions, garlic, and ginger. Form into meatballs.
3. **Bake Meatballs**: Place on a baking sheet and bake for 20 minutes.
4. **Prepare Glaze**: In a saucepan, combine soy sauce, honey, and sesame oil. Simmer until thickened.
5. **Coat Meatballs**: Toss baked meatballs in the soy glaze before serving. Garnish with sesame seeds.

Cheese and Charcuterie Board

Ingredients:

- Assorted cheeses (cheddar, brie, gouda)
- Cured meats (salami, prosciutto, chorizo)
- Crackers and bread
- Fresh fruits (grapes, figs, apple slices)
- Nuts (almonds, walnuts)
- Olives and pickles
- Honey or fruit preserves

Instructions:

1. **Arrange Ingredients**: On a large board or platter, arrange cheeses and cured meats.
2. **Add Accompaniments**: Fill in gaps with crackers, fruits, nuts, olives, and pickles.
3. **Serve**: Drizzle with honey or add fruit preserves for a sweet touch.

Mini Tacos with Avocado Salsa

Ingredients:

- 12 mini corn tortillas
- 1 lb ground beef or turkey
- 1 packet taco seasoning
- 1 avocado, diced
- 1/2 cup cherry tomatoes, diced
- 1/4 cup red onion, chopped
- Lime juice (to taste)
- Cilantro (for garnish)

Instructions:

1. **Cook Meat**: In a skillet, cook ground meat with taco seasoning according to package instructions.
2. **Make Salsa**: In a bowl, combine avocado, tomatoes, red onion, lime juice, and cilantro.
3. **Assemble Tacos**: Fill each mini tortilla with cooked meat and top with avocado salsa.
4. **Serve**: Enjoy fresh!

Sweet Potato Bites with Maple Glaze

Ingredients:

- 2 medium sweet potatoes, sliced into rounds
- 2 tablespoons olive oil
- Salt and pepper (to taste)
- 1/4 cup maple syrup
- Chopped pecans (for garnish)

Instructions:

1. **Preheat the Oven**: Preheat to 425°F (220°C).
2. **Prepare Sweet Potatoes**: Toss sweet potato rounds with olive oil, salt, and pepper. Spread on a baking sheet.
3. **Bake**: Roast for 20-25 minutes until tender.
4. **Glaze**: Drizzle with maple syrup and sprinkle with chopped pecans before serving.

Hummus and Veggie Cups

Ingredients:

- 1 cup hummus (store-bought or homemade)
- Assorted veggies (carrot sticks, cucumber slices, bell pepper strips, cherry tomatoes)
- Small cups or jars

Instructions:

1. **Portion Hummus**: Place a few tablespoons of hummus at the bottom of each cup.
2. **Add Veggies**: Arrange veggie sticks in each cup.
3. **Serve**: Enjoy as a healthy and colorful snack!

Smoked Salmon and Cream Cheese Wraps

Ingredients:

- 4 large tortillas or wraps
- 8 oz cream cheese, softened
- 8 oz smoked salmon
- Fresh dill (for garnish)
- Capers (optional)

Instructions:

1. **Spread Cream Cheese**: Spread a layer of cream cheese over each tortilla.
2. **Add Salmon**: Lay smoked salmon on top and sprinkle with fresh dill and capers.
3. **Roll and Slice**: Roll each tortilla tightly and slice into pinwheels.
4. **Serve**: Enjoy chilled!

Mini Caprese Salad Cups

Ingredients:

- Cherry tomatoes, halved
- Fresh mozzarella balls (bocconcini)
- Fresh basil leaves
- Balsamic glaze
- Small cups or skewers

Instructions:

1. **Assemble Cups**: In each cup, layer halved cherry tomatoes, mozzarella balls, and basil leaves.
2. **Drizzle**: Add a drizzle of balsamic glaze on top.
3. **Serve**: Enjoy as a refreshing bite!

Thai Chicken Satay Skewers

Ingredients:

- 1 lb chicken breast, cut into strips
- 1/4 cup soy sauce
- 2 tablespoons peanut butter
- 1 tablespoon honey
- 1 tablespoon lime juice
- Skewers (soaked in water if wooden)

Instructions:

1. **Marinate Chicken**: In a bowl, whisk together soy sauce, peanut butter, honey, and lime juice. Marinate chicken strips for at least 30 minutes.
2. **Skewer Chicken**: Thread marinated chicken onto skewers.
3. **Grill or Bake**: Grill for 5-7 minutes per side or bake at 400°F (200°C) for 15-20 minutes.
4. **Serve**: Enjoy with a peanut dipping sauce if desired.

Enjoy these delicious appetizers at your next gathering!

Mini Grilled Cheese Sandwiches

Ingredients:

- 8 slices of bread (white or whole grain)
- 4 oz cheddar cheese, sliced
- 4 oz mozzarella cheese, sliced
- Butter (for grilling)

Instructions:

1. **Prepare Sandwiches**: Assemble sandwiches by placing slices of cheddar and mozzarella between two slices of bread.
2. **Butter Bread**: Spread butter on the outer sides of each sandwich.
3. **Grill**: Heat a skillet over medium heat. Grill sandwiches until golden brown and cheese is melted, about 3-4 minutes per side.
4. **Slice and Serve**: Cut into quarters and serve warm.

Jalapeño Poppers with Cream Cheese

Ingredients:

- 12 jalapeños, halved and seeded
- 8 oz cream cheese, softened
- 1/2 cup shredded cheddar cheese
- 1/4 teaspoon garlic powder
- 1/4 teaspoon smoked paprika
- Bacon bits (optional)

Instructions:

1. **Preheat the Oven**: Preheat to 375°F (190°C).
2. **Mix Filling**: In a bowl, combine cream cheese, cheddar cheese, garlic powder, and smoked paprika.
3. **Stuff Jalapeños**: Fill each jalapeño half with the cream cheese mixture. Top with bacon bits if desired.
4. **Bake**: Place on a baking sheet and bake for 20-25 minutes until bubbly and golden.
5. **Serve**: Enjoy warm!

Olive Tapenade on Crostini

Ingredients:

- 1 cup mixed olives, pitted
- 2 tablespoons capers
- 2 cloves garlic
- 1/4 cup olive oil
- Baguette, sliced and toasted

Instructions:

1. **Make Tapenade**: In a food processor, combine olives, capers, garlic, and olive oil. Blend until chunky.
2. **Prepare Crostini**: Toast baguette slices until golden.
3. **Top Crostini**: Spread olive tapenade on toasted baguette slices.
4. **Serve**: Enjoy as an elegant appetizer!

Buffalo Cauliflower Bites

Ingredients:

- 1 head cauliflower, cut into florets
- 1 cup flour
- 1 cup water
- 1 cup buffalo sauce
- Olive oil (for drizzling)

Instructions:

1. **Preheat the Oven**: Preheat to 450°F (230°C).
2. **Make Batter**: In a bowl, mix flour, water, and a pinch of salt to create a batter.
3. **Coat Cauliflower**: Dip cauliflower florets into the batter and place on a baking sheet.
4. **Bake**: Bake for 20 minutes until crispy.
5. **Toss in Sauce**: Remove from the oven, toss with buffalo sauce, and return to the oven for an additional 10 minutes.
6. **Serve**: Enjoy warm!

Mini Quiches Lorraine

Ingredients:

- 6 large eggs
- 1 cup heavy cream
- 1/2 cup cooked bacon, chopped
- 1/2 cup shredded Swiss cheese
- 1/4 teaspoon salt
- 1/4 teaspoon pepper
- 1 package mini pastry shells or phyllo cups

Instructions:

1. **Preheat the Oven**: Preheat to 375°F (190°C).
2. **Whisk Ingredients**: In a bowl, whisk together eggs, cream, salt, and pepper.
3. **Fill Cups**: Place bacon and cheese in each pastry shell, then pour the egg mixture on top.
4. **Bake**: Bake for 20-25 minutes until set and golden.
5. **Serve**: Enjoy warm!

Sesame Crusted Ahi Tuna Bites

Ingredients:

- 1 lb ahi tuna, cut into cubes
- 1/4 cup sesame seeds
- 2 tablespoons soy sauce
- 1 tablespoon olive oil
- Green onions (for garnish)

Instructions:

1. **Coat Tuna**: In a bowl, toss tuna cubes with soy sauce. Roll in sesame seeds to coat.
2. **Sear Tuna**: Heat olive oil in a skillet over high heat. Sear tuna for about 1 minute on each side.
3. **Slice and Serve**: Remove from heat, slice, and garnish with green onions. Serve immediately.

Roasted Red Pepper Hummus Pinwheels

Ingredients:

- 1 large tortilla
- 1/2 cup roasted red pepper hummus
- 1/2 cup fresh spinach leaves
- 1/4 cup feta cheese, crumbled

Instructions:

1. **Spread Hummus**: Spread hummus evenly over the tortilla.
2. **Layer Ingredients**: Top with spinach and feta cheese.
3. **Roll and Slice**: Roll the tortilla tightly and slice into pinwheels.
4. **Serve**: Enjoy as a tasty snack!

Cheesy Garlic Breadsticks

Ingredients:

- 1 package pizza dough
- 4 tablespoons butter, melted
- 2 cloves garlic, minced
- 1 cup shredded mozzarella cheese
- Italian seasoning (for garnish)

Instructions:

1. **Preheat the Oven**: Preheat to 400°F (200°C).
2. **Prepare Dough**: Roll out pizza dough on a baking sheet into a rectangle.
3. **Brush with Butter**: Mix melted butter and garlic, then brush over the dough.
4. **Add Cheese**: Sprinkle mozzarella cheese on top and garnish with Italian seasoning.
5. **Bake**: Bake for 15-20 minutes until golden and bubbly.
6. **Slice and Serve**: Cut into sticks and enjoy warm!

Enjoy these delightful appetizers at your next gathering!

Coconut Shrimp with Mango Dipping Sauce

Ingredients:

- 1 lb large shrimp, peeled and deveined
- 1 cup shredded coconut
- 1/2 cup breadcrumbs
- 2 eggs, beaten
- 1 cup flour
- Oil (for frying)

For Mango Dipping Sauce:

- 1 ripe mango, diced
- 2 tablespoons lime juice
- Salt (to taste)

Instructions:

1. **Prepare Dipping Sauce**: In a blender, combine mango, lime juice, and salt. Blend until smooth. Set aside.
2. **Coat Shrimp**: Dredge shrimp in flour, dip in beaten eggs, then coat with a mixture of shredded coconut and breadcrumbs.
3. **Fry Shrimp**: Heat oil in a pan over medium heat. Fry shrimp for 2-3 minutes on each side until golden brown.
4. **Serve**: Plate shrimp with mango dipping sauce on the side.

Tomato Basil Bruschetta with Balsamic Glaze

Ingredients:

- 1 baguette, sliced
- 2 cups diced tomatoes
- 1/4 cup fresh basil, chopped
- 2 cloves garlic, minced
- 2 tablespoons olive oil
- Balsamic glaze (for drizzling)

Instructions:

1. **Toast Bread**: Preheat oven to 400°F (200°C). Toast baguette slices on a baking sheet for 5-7 minutes.
2. **Mix Topping**: In a bowl, combine tomatoes, basil, garlic, olive oil, salt, and pepper.
3. **Top Bread**: Spoon the tomato mixture onto toasted baguette slices.
4. **Drizzle and Serve**: Drizzle with balsamic glaze before serving.

Antipasto Skewers

Ingredients:

- Cherry tomatoes
- Mozzarella balls (bocconcini)
- Salami slices
- Kalamata olives
- Fresh basil leaves
- Skewers

Instructions:

1. **Assemble Skewers**: On each skewer, thread a cherry tomato, a mozzarella ball, a folded salami slice, an olive, and a basil leaf. Repeat until filled.
2. **Serve**: Arrange on a platter and enjoy as a colorful appetizer!

Mini BBQ Chicken Sliders

Ingredients:

- 2 cups shredded cooked chicken
- 1/2 cup BBQ sauce
- Slider buns
- Pickles (for topping)

Instructions:

1. **Mix Chicken**: In a bowl, combine shredded chicken with BBQ sauce until well coated.
2. **Assemble Sliders**: Place a spoonful of BBQ chicken on each slider bun. Top with pickles.
3. **Serve**: Enjoy warm or at room temperature!

Cucumber Bites with Dill Cream Cheese

Ingredients:

- 1 large cucumber, sliced
- 8 oz cream cheese, softened
- 2 tablespoons fresh dill, chopped
- Salt and pepper (to taste)

Instructions:

1. **Mix Cream Cheese**: In a bowl, combine cream cheese, dill, salt, and pepper until smooth.
2. **Top Cucumbers**: Spread a dollop of cream cheese mixture on each cucumber slice.
3. **Serve**: Enjoy as a refreshing snack!

Spicy Tuna Tartare on Wonton Chips

Ingredients:

- 1 lb sushi-grade tuna, diced
- 2 tablespoons soy sauce
- 1 tablespoon sesame oil
- 1 tablespoon Sriracha (adjust to taste)
- Wonton chips
- Green onions (for garnish)

Instructions:

1. **Mix Tuna**: In a bowl, combine diced tuna, soy sauce, sesame oil, and Sriracha. Toss to coat.
2. **Prepare Wonton Chips**: Bake or fry wonton wrappers until crispy.
3. **Assemble**: Place a spoonful of tuna tartare on each wonton chip and garnish with chopped green onions.
4. **Serve**: Enjoy immediately!

Eggplant Caponata on Crostini

Ingredients:

- 1 large eggplant, diced
- 1/2 cup onion, chopped
- 1/2 cup celery, chopped
- 1/4 cup olives, chopped
- 1/4 cup capers
- 1/4 cup balsamic vinegar
- Crostini (toasted baguette slices)

Instructions:

1. **Cook Eggplant**: In a skillet, sauté eggplant, onion, and celery until softened.
2. **Add Other Ingredients**: Stir in olives, capers, and balsamic vinegar. Cook for another 5 minutes.
3. **Top Crostini**: Spoon eggplant caponata onto toasted crostini.
4. **Serve**: Enjoy warm or at room temperature!

Parmesan Crisps with Whipped Goat Cheese

Ingredients:

- 1 cup grated Parmesan cheese
- 4 oz goat cheese, softened
- 2 tablespoons cream (or milk)
- Fresh herbs (for garnish)

Instructions:

1. **Make Parmesan Crisps**: Preheat oven to 400°F (200°C). Line a baking sheet with parchment paper. Place small mounds of grated Parmesan on the sheet and bake for 5-7 minutes until golden.
2. **Whip Goat Cheese**: In a bowl, whisk together goat cheese and cream until smooth.
3. **Assemble**: Let crisps cool slightly, then top each with a dollop of whipped goat cheese.
4. **Garnish and Serve**: Sprinkle with fresh herbs before serving.

Enjoy these delicious appetizers at your next gathering!

Caramelized Onion and Gruyère Tartlets

Ingredients:

- 1 sheet puff pastry, thawed
- 2 large onions, thinly sliced
- 1 cup Gruyère cheese, shredded
- 2 tablespoons olive oil
- 1 tablespoon balsamic vinegar
- Salt and pepper (to taste)
- Fresh thyme (for garnish)

Instructions:

1. **Preheat the Oven**: Preheat to 400°F (200°C).
2. **Caramelize Onions**: In a skillet, heat olive oil over medium heat. Add onions and cook until soft and caramelized, about 15-20 minutes. Stir in balsamic vinegar, salt, and pepper.
3. **Prepare Pastry**: Roll out puff pastry and cut into squares. Place squares on a baking sheet lined with parchment paper.
4. **Fill Tartlets**: Spoon caramelized onions onto each pastry square and sprinkle with Gruyère cheese.
5. **Bake**: Bake for 15-20 minutes until golden brown and puffed.
6. **Serve**: Garnish with fresh thyme before serving warm.

Zucchini Fritters with Yogurt Sauce

Ingredients:

- 2 medium zucchinis, grated
- 1/2 cup flour
- 2 large eggs
- 1/4 cup grated Parmesan cheese
- Salt and pepper (to taste)
- Oil (for frying)

For Yogurt Sauce:

- 1 cup Greek yogurt
- 1 tablespoon lemon juice
- 1 clove garlic, minced
- Salt (to taste)

Instructions:

1. **Prepare Fritters**: In a bowl, mix grated zucchini with flour, eggs, Parmesan, salt, and pepper. Form mixture into patties.
2. **Fry Fritters**: Heat oil in a skillet over medium heat. Fry fritters for about 3-4 minutes on each side until golden brown.
3. **Make Yogurt Sauce**: In another bowl, mix yogurt, lemon juice, garlic, and salt.
4. **Serve**: Plate fritters with a dollop of yogurt sauce on the side.

Fruit and Cheese Skewers

Ingredients:

- Assorted cheeses (cheddar, brie, gouda)
- Fresh fruits (grapes, strawberries, apple slices)
- Skewers

Instructions:

1. **Assemble Skewers**: On each skewer, thread pieces of cheese and fruit in an alternating pattern.
2. **Serve**: Arrange on a platter for a colorful and refreshing appetizer!

Curried Chicken Salad in Endive Leaves

Ingredients:

- 2 cups cooked chicken, shredded
- 1/4 cup mayonnaise
- 1 tablespoon curry powder
- 1/4 cup diced apples
- 1/4 cup raisins
- Salt and pepper (to taste)
- Endive leaves

Instructions:

1. **Make Chicken Salad**: In a bowl, combine shredded chicken, mayonnaise, curry powder, apples, raisins, salt, and pepper.
2. **Prepare Endive Leaves**: Gently separate endive leaves and rinse.
3. **Fill Leaves**: Spoon chicken salad into each endive leaf.
4. **Serve**: Enjoy as a crunchy, flavorful bite!

Baked Brie with Cranberries and Pecans

Ingredients:

- 1 wheel of Brie cheese
- 1/2 cup cranberries (dried or fresh)
- 1/4 cup pecans, chopped
- 2 tablespoons honey
- Fresh rosemary (for garnish)
- Crackers (for serving)

Instructions:

1. **Preheat the Oven**: Preheat to 350°F (175°C).
2. **Prepare Brie**: Place Brie on a baking dish. Top with cranberries, pecans, and drizzle with honey.
3. **Bake**: Bake for 15-20 minutes until melty.
4. **Serve**: Garnish with fresh rosemary and serve with crackers.

Mini Corn Dogs with Mustard Dip

Ingredients:

- 1 cup cornmeal
- 1 cup flour
- 1 tablespoon baking powder
- 1 cup buttermilk
- 1 egg
- Mini hot dogs
- Oil (for frying)

For Mustard Dip:

- 1/4 cup mustard
- 1 tablespoon honey

Instructions:

1. **Prepare Batter**: In a bowl, mix cornmeal, flour, baking powder, buttermilk, and egg until smooth.
2. **Heat Oil**: In a pot, heat oil over medium heat.
3. **Dip Hot Dogs**: Dip mini hot dogs into the batter and fry until golden brown, about 3-4 minutes.
4. **Make Mustard Dip**: In a small bowl, combine mustard and honey.
5. **Serve**: Plate corn dogs with mustard dip on the side.

Roasted Garlic and White Bean Dip

Ingredients:

- 1 head garlic
- 1 can (15 oz) white beans, drained and rinsed
- 2 tablespoons olive oil
- 1 tablespoon lemon juice
- Salt and pepper (to taste)
- Fresh parsley (for garnish)

Instructions:

1. **Roast Garlic**: Preheat oven to 400°F (200°C). Wrap garlic head in foil and roast for 30-35 minutes until soft.
2. **Make Dip**: Squeeze roasted garlic into a food processor. Add white beans, olive oil, lemon juice, salt, and pepper. Blend until smooth.
3. **Serve**: Transfer to a bowl, garnish with parsley, and serve with pita chips or vegetables.

Veggie Spring Rolls with Peanut Dipping Sauce

Ingredients:

- Rice paper wrappers
- Assorted vegetables (carrots, bell peppers, cucumber, lettuce)
- Fresh herbs (mint, cilantro)
- 1/2 cup peanut butter
- 2 tablespoons soy sauce
- 1 tablespoon lime juice

Instructions:

1. **Prepare Filling**: Julienne vegetables and set aside.
2. **Soak Rice Paper**: Soak rice paper wrappers in warm water until pliable.
3. **Assemble Rolls**: Lay a wrapper flat, add a mix of vegetables and herbs, then roll tightly.
4. **Make Peanut Sauce**: In a bowl, whisk together peanut butter, soy sauce, and lime juice until smooth.
5. **Serve**: Plate spring rolls with peanut dipping sauce on the side.

Enjoy these delicious appetizers at your next gathering!

Mini Pesto and Mozzarella Flatbreads

Ingredients:

- 1 package store-bought flatbread or pizza dough
- 1/2 cup pesto sauce
- 1 cup fresh mozzarella, sliced
- Cherry tomatoes, halved
- Olive oil (for drizzling)
- Fresh basil (for garnish)

Instructions:

1. **Preheat the Oven**: Preheat to 400°F (200°C).
2. **Prepare Flatbreads**: Place flatbreads on a baking sheet. Spread pesto evenly over each.
3. **Add Toppings**: Top with mozzarella slices and cherry tomato halves.
4. **Bake**: Bake for 10-12 minutes until cheese is bubbly and golden.
5. **Serve**: Drizzle with olive oil and garnish with fresh basil before serving.

Sweet and Spicy Meatballs

Ingredients:

- 1 lb ground beef or turkey
- 1/2 cup breadcrumbs
- 1/4 cup onion, finely chopped
- 1 egg
- 1/4 cup sweet chili sauce
- 1/4 cup soy sauce
- 1 tablespoon honey
- 1 teaspoon sriracha (adjust to taste)

Instructions:

1. **Preheat the Oven**: Preheat to 375°F (190°C).
2. **Mix Ingredients**: In a bowl, combine ground meat, breadcrumbs, onion, and egg. Form into meatballs.
3. **Bake Meatballs**: Place on a baking sheet and bake for 20-25 minutes until cooked through.
4. **Make Sauce**: In a saucepan, mix sweet chili sauce, soy sauce, honey, and sriracha. Heat until warm.
5. **Coat Meatballs**: Toss baked meatballs in the sauce and serve warm.

Mushroom and Swiss Sliders

Ingredients:

- 1 lb ground beef
- 1 cup mushrooms, finely chopped
- 1/2 cup Swiss cheese, shredded
- 1 tablespoon Worcestershire sauce
- Slider buns
- Olive oil (for cooking)
- Salt and pepper (to taste)

Instructions:

1. **Sauté Mushrooms**: In a skillet, heat olive oil and sauté mushrooms until tender. Set aside.
2. **Mix Beef**: In a bowl, combine ground beef, sautéed mushrooms, Worcestershire sauce, salt, and pepper. Form into slider patties.
3. **Cook Patties**: Grill or pan-fry patties for 3-4 minutes on each side until cooked to your liking. Top with Swiss cheese and cover until melted.
4. **Assemble Sliders**: Place patties on slider buns and serve.

Chocolate-Dipped Strawberries

Ingredients:

- 1 lb fresh strawberries, washed and dried
- 8 oz semi-sweet chocolate, chopped
- White chocolate (for drizzling, optional)

Instructions:

1. **Melt Chocolate**: In a microwave-safe bowl, melt semi-sweet chocolate in 30-second intervals until smooth.
2. **Dip Strawberries**: Dip each strawberry into the melted chocolate, allowing excess to drip off.
3. **Cool**: Place on a parchment-lined baking sheet. Refrigerate until chocolate is set.
4. **Drizzle (Optional)**: Melt white chocolate and drizzle over set strawberries for decoration.
5. **Serve**: Enjoy fresh!

Avocado Deviled Eggs

Ingredients:

- 6 large eggs, hard-boiled and peeled
- 1 ripe avocado
- 1 tablespoon lime juice
- 1/4 teaspoon garlic powder
- Salt and pepper (to taste)
- Paprika (for garnish)

Instructions:

1. **Prepare Eggs**: Slice hard-boiled eggs in half and remove yolks.
2. **Make Filling**: In a bowl, mash yolks with avocado, lime juice, garlic powder, salt, and pepper until smooth.
3. **Fill Eggs**: Spoon or pipe the avocado mixture back into the egg whites.
4. **Garnish**: Sprinkle with paprika before serving.

Beet and Goat Cheese Salad Bites

Ingredients:

- 2 medium beets, roasted and sliced
- 4 oz goat cheese, softened
- Fresh arugula or spinach
- Balsamic glaze (for drizzling)
- Salt and pepper (to taste)

Instructions:

1. **Prepare Bites**: On a serving platter, layer beet slices with a small dollop of goat cheese and a few arugula leaves.
2. **Drizzle**: Lightly drizzle with balsamic glaze and season with salt and pepper.
3. **Serve**: Enjoy as a vibrant, flavorful bite!

Lemon Basil Shrimp Cups

Ingredients:

- 1 lb shrimp, peeled and deveined
- 2 tablespoons olive oil
- 2 tablespoons lemon juice
- 1/4 cup fresh basil, chopped
- Mini phyllo cups or lettuce leaves

Instructions:

1. **Cook Shrimp**: In a skillet, heat olive oil over medium heat. Add shrimp, lemon juice, salt, and pepper. Cook until shrimp are pink and opaque, about 3-4 minutes.
2. **Mix with Basil**: Remove from heat and stir in chopped basil.
3. **Assemble Cups**: Spoon shrimp mixture into mini phyllo cups or serve in lettuce leaves.
4. **Serve**: Enjoy warm or at room temperature!

Enjoy these delicious appetizers at your next gathering!